8 REASONS
CHRISTIANS SHOULDN'T DRINK

Other books by Michael W. H. Holcomb

The First Five Words

If the Bible Taught the Trinity, I'd Believe It

Baptized Into the Lord Jesus Christ

Attainable Perfection

Conscious

8 REASONS CHRISTIANS SHOULDN'T DRINK

MICHAEL W. H. HOLCOMB

BIBLEDAYS
MINISTRIES

8 REASONS CHRISTIANS SHOULDN'T DRINK

Copyright © 2012
Michael W. H. Holcomb
www.bibledays.org

Published by BibleDays Ministries
PO Box 2515
Williamsport, PA 17703

ISBN 978-0-9837858-5-9

Printed in the United States of America by instantpublisher.com

All quotes from the Bible are taken from the King James Version.

The author uses an *upper style* for religious writing, capitalizing the eternal places, nouns and pronouns that refer to God, the word *Church* (when it denotes the world-wide body of believers), and other biblical terminology.

To Pastors Dan and Kim Barker

TABLE OF CONTENTS

Foreword

O ver the last few years (and after several conver-
sations about the subject), a number of people
have asked me to write a book about what I have
found in statistics and in the Bible concerning alcohol. Apparently, many Christians are convinced it is
wrong for them personally; and in addition, they
know that a great number of churches have a standard against it, they see what it does to others, and
they can recall that the Bible has a lot of negative
things to say about drinking let alone drunkenness.
However, these same ones feel ill-equipped to answer prevailing questions on the subject, especially
as it pertains to fellow believers.

One reason for this is that the majority of arguments supporting "Christian drinking" are based on
half-truths, speculation, and look-who-else-does-it
inferences, none of which are immediately verifiable
and cannot, therefore, be satisfactorily negated by

the unstudied. Another reason people find it difficult to respond is that those who defend indulging in alcoholic beverages are quick to pronounce the topic a scriptural "gray area," simply because they find no verse that says something like, "Thou shalt not drink alcohol." This seemingly impenetrable position is particularly intimidating.

My response to all of this is that the biblical mandates God so wisely requires of His children practically rule out the question of drinking (I say "practically" because there is one exception the Bible makes for drinking: medicinal purposes, but even that, as you will discover, is rigidly defined.). In other words, no commandment directly against alcohol is needed; and neither the prognostications about ancient wines nor any other "pro-drinking" justification have legitimate grounds. What Christians are forbidden to do and how we are told to behave makes all the fuss null and void. It's that simple!

In making this statement, I do not imply, in anyway, that scientific or scholarly approaches are without merit. I have read and benefitted from some fine articles and books by those to whom God has given their own "take" on the subject of abstinence. Indeed, I would encourage all those who read this book to educate themselves on how ancient Hebrews made and used the "fruit of the vine" as I found the study to weaken arguments for drinking.

My hope is simply to contribute to the case a manual of a few but rock-solid biblical principles that will satisfy personal questions and that will arm pastors, parents, and saints everywhere with concrete answers. I want to see every believer be strong in Christ Jesus, without the lies, pressures, or hindrances of the modern infatuation with alcohol. Therefore, I submit the following work to my brothers and sisters in Christ Jesus for their pursuit of holiness and for the glory of Almighty God.

I would especially like to extend much thanks to David McKernan for proofreading the rough draft for this book—and on such short notice, too. God bless you, brother!

Michael W. H. Holcomb
Williamsport, PA

PART ONE

GET REAL!

CHAPTER ONE

Alcohol is a Problem

L et's get something straight, right now. *Alcohol is an enormous problem*!

I was at a local college the other day, and walking by some of the administrative offices, I noticed a large plexiglass display of free literature. I counted 10 different pamphlets about alcohol. It was the most addressed topic! Why? Because for many people, alcohol has been *the* reason for …

- Legal trouble.
- Sexually transmitted diseases.
- Regrettable as well as humiliating behavior.
- Financial problems.
- The inability to obtain a professional occupation or even retain the simplest of jobs.
- Deterioration of skills and learning.

- Broken trust and shattered respect in every kind of relationship.

The individual difficulties caused by alcohol are impossible to track; however, if you want to talk about "social issues," there are other data gauges that shed light on the enormity of what ought to be considered an alcohol crisis. The National Institute on Alcohol Abuse and Alcoholism estimates that in the United States "about 18 million people have an alcohol use disorder;"[1] however, only 24% of them get treatment.[2] That means millions who ought to be in rehabilitation programs or getting some other kind of help are walking around in absolute denial!

On their FAQs and Facts webpage, the National Council of Alcoholism and Drug Prevention writes,

One in every 12 adults, suffer from alcohol abuse or dependence along with several million more who engage in risky, binge drinking patterns that could lead to alcohol problems. More than half of all adults have a family history of alcoholism or problem drinking, and more than 7 million children live in a household where at least one parent is dependent on or has abused alcohol.[3]

According to the World Health Organization, alcohol kills 2.5 million people a year;[4] and in the United States, excessive alcohol use is the 3rd leading lifestyle-related cause of death.[5] Approximately 6,000 teens die annually from drinking alcohol. That is more adolescent deaths than from all illegal drugs put together![6] Furthermore, the WHO publication, *Child Maltreatment and Alcohol*, opens up with the statement, "Strong links have been found between child maltreatment and alcohol use."[7] The Centers for Disease Control and Prevention calculated that in 2010 intoxicated adults got behind the wheel 112 million times, which translates to 300,000 a day,[8] while in the same year, the National Highway Traffic Safety Administration reported there were 10,228 fatalities due to drunk driving.[9] That is 28 dead people per day.

The National Institute on Drug Abuse has reported that high school students who drink or use other substances are five times more likely either to become a drop out or to form the opinion that good grades are unimportant.[10] Additionally, in its most recent study (1999), the Department of Health and Human Services estimated that alcohol abuse was responsible for $191.6 billion in social costs.[11]

17

The statistics go on and on and on; but just the fact that there are multiple branches of Federal and State governments devoted to controlling or following up on alcohol should indicate the scope of danger and difficulties attributed to drinking!

THE EUROPEAN MYTH

I was in Germany a number of years ago holding special meetings with a group of other American preachers. After one of the services, the pastor took the ministry team out to eat at a local pizzeria. After all of us sat down, the pastor leaned into the table and said to us in a determined voice, "You are not in America anymore, and I want you to know that you can order *anything* you want from the menu. It's okay." He was not primarily talking about the food items. He was talking about alcoholic beverages. Of course, we on the ministry team ordered soda.

Ironically, as the pastor began indulging in his beer, wine, and sherry—all this just during our "late night bite"—a quiet young man from the church, who was sitting across from me, introduced himself and then unexpectedly said, "I don't drink. I was raised in an alcoholic home."

This young man's personal protest took me aback. "Wait a minute!" I thought to myself. "Back home, one excuse church kids have for drinking is that in Europe, where drinking is much more culturally acceptable and where almost all Christians drink, people have learned how to handle their booze. Now here is a guy telling me that he doesn't even drink in moderation because he has seen the horrors of alcohol!"

Contrary to what rumors had trained me to believe, I later found out this young man's scenario was not an isolated, rare one. In April 2011, the German Centre for Addiction Issues (DHS) released a shocking report that *one in five Germans has a drinking problem*! Director for the Centre, Raphael Gaßmann, said, "Alcohol consumption remains conspicuously too high, too risky, with too many consequences." Gaßmann also noted that their results on binge drinking were "dramatic" and noticeably worse.[12] Deutsche Welle (a German broadcasting company) had already reported in November 2007 that it was not just teens but "a full 34 percent of adults binge drink daily."[13] Only four years later, that percentage was higher! DW had also carried an article in which they quoted from Peter Lang, head of Drug Prevention and Abuse at the German Center for Health Education, "Alcoholism is a significant problem in Germany." According to the same article:

> 1.7 million Germans are dependent on alcohol and need treatment, whilst, 2.7 million use alcohol in a harmful way.[14]

In 2005, leading French journalist, Hervé Chabalier (a former alcoholic), presented a report to Health Minister Xavier Bertrand entitled, *Alcoholism - The Simple Truth*. The report showed that alcohol was directly responsible for 23,000 deaths a year in France, indirectly responsible for another 22,000, and while 5 million people were found to be drinking too much, 2 million were alcoholics. Chabalier's report also noted that half of all domestic violence was due to alcohol.[15] Also according to Chabalier, France has always culturally just seen "the good side of alcohol" while ignoring its problems.

A year ago I was in an Amsterdam book store when the title, *Onze Kinderen En Alcohol* (Our Children on Alcohol), caught my eye. This book correlated with a Dutch study that was recently conducted by Selma Bouthoorn, Joris van Hoof, and Nicolaas van der Lely in which they reported, "Alcohol intoxication among adolescents is an emerging problem ... The number of adolescents admitted [to

Dutch hospitals] with alcohol intoxication increased sharply from 2007 to 2009."[16]

Documents from the British government in 2007-08 show that alcohol use of some kind was connected to more than a million of their crimes,[17] and according to the 2009-10 BCS, "victims believed the offender(s) to be under the influence of alcohol in half (50%) of all violent incidents."[18] Here is an eye-opener: the 2010-11 Scottish Crime and Justice Survey found that 74% of Scots think alcohol abuse in Scotland is "a bigger problem than crime, anti-social behaviour and unemployment."[19]

People are people, and alcohol affects everyone the same way, no matter the culture to which we belong.

WHAT GOES UNNOTICED

Keep in mind, none of these facts and figures include what every pastor, social worker, and police officer in the world finds to be the other all too common ills. What about the countless marriages alcohol has ruined? What about the fighting and violence that regularly erupt in bars, streets, private gatherings, and homes because of alcohol? What about the physical abuse of spouses and children for which alcohol is responsible? What about the attempted suicides or the rape and incest cases involving alcohol which never get reported (the ones we, who work with the public, find out about long after they have happened)? On top of all this, we have yet to talk of the fornication, adultery, debauchery, drunkenness, and all the other abominations that are a familiar and frequent part of alcohol's ungodly subculture!

I have met a few Christians who say we should not drink caffeine because it is fleshly and has an unholy effect on us, but this is a pathetic belief and I will tell you why. Caffeine is in no way connected with sin, neither is caffeine a troublemaker. I know of no one who has gotten into a car wreck because of driving under the influence of caffeine. Drinking caffeine does not lead to fornication or beating your kids or out-of-control behavior. There are no recovery homes for those who drink caffeine, and no one is signing up for caffeine drinkers anonymous—but the same cannot be said of alcohol!

"Wine is a mocker," Proverbs 20:1 says. Alcohol promises fun, it promises class, it promises to give you the reputation of being a cool guy or a "with-it" girl; and to many people, it even promises an air of intelligence. Yet the fancy bottles and the sophisticated, high-tech commercials all lure people into a world that gets shockingly ugly, shockingly fast.

What really troubles me is the way alcohol, and by extension the devil, is making a mockery of Christians. In my twenty plus years of being a pastor and a traveling preacher, I have seen and heard of disaster after disaster, church folks (preachers included) who thought they could beat the odds and drink without being affected spiritually; but how wrong they have been! Many times I have gone to churches to minister and, upon stepping through the door, have sensed by the Holy Ghost an atmosphere of spiritual deadness and intense carnality; and almost every time, I have learned that somebody in leadership has, among other things, opened the door to alcohol. Some of what I have personally encountered I share in the pages of this book, but I have to wonder: If I, only one minister, am seeing such a huge mess, what is the overall damage? It must be staggering!

SEE THE WHOLE TRUTH

I have a suggestion for all those who market alcohol. How about taking a drive down our nation's "bad parts of town" and reporting on what alcohol has done to countless people? How about advertising beer and liquor using those who are their biggest fans: the foul-smelling man huddled in the alley, clutching onto his inseparable wine bottle; the dys-functional mother sleeping in till noon because of another hangover; the flunking college student sit-ting in a counselor's office after another weekend of getting stoned? Along with all the taste awards, why not put on the wine bottles the number of homes that particular vintage has broken or the number of auto-accidents it has caused? Instead of showing young, smiling, *sober* models with a drink in their hand, how about showing the whole truth!?

Of course I am being facetious, but am I being any worse than those who are self-deceived about alcohol? The myriad of problems and deadly draw-backs brought about by alcohol are like the proverbi-al elephant in the room everyone pretends not to notice—and in my opinion, church people seem to be the worst at this denial!

Christians who start asking about "drinking in moderation" had better be ready to face the disturb-ing facts about alcohol as well as face what the Bible clearly teaches concerning Christian conduct. Alco-holic drinks are not just another beverage. They cer-tainly have no intrinsic connection to maturity, and they do far more—dangerously more—than identify you with your culture or your ideal lifestyle. Where there is alcohol, there is trouble—serious trouble and lots of it. But then again, that stands to reason when we consider the following chapter.

CHAPTER TWO

Alcohol is a Drug

The United States Department of Health and Human Services says it best:

Alcohol is a drug, as surely as cocaine and marijuana are ... [it is] powerful, mood-altering ... [and] slows down the body and mind. It impairs coordination; slows reaction time; and impairs vision, clear thinking, and judgment.[1]

Unlike food, alcohol is immediately absorbed into your blood stream; and *within 90 seconds*, it affects every organ and body system. It even crosses the blood-brain barrier, which normally keeps unsafe substances from the brain.[2] Though people may not feel drunk, the relaxed and contented feeling that comes after the first drink indicates an immediate loss of some of their judgment.[3] Nick Gilmore of the

Army Substance Abuse Program, commenting on a recent study by ASAP, said:

> One of the effects of alcohol is it lowers inhibitions and allows the user to relax. Alcohol abuse allows users to relax to the point of not considering the consequences of their behavior ...[4]

General Barry McCaffrey, former Director of the Office of National Drug Control Policy (1996-2001), once said, "The most dangerous drug in America today is still alcohol;"[5] and U. S. News and World Report ran a June 2012 article reporting that,

> "Drug harms in the UK: a multi-criteria decision analysis", a 2010 study from the Independent Scientific Committee on Drugs published in The Lancet (and reported on by multiplemedia outlets) is very clear about which drugs are most harmful.

> The study placed heroin, crack and meth far above marijuana, both in terms of harm to self and harm to others. Cocaine and tobacco were also ranked as more harmful than marijuana. <u>Alcohol was ranked most dangerous.</u>[6]

You read right: Alcohol had more "harm scores" than marijuana, cocaine, heroin, crack, or even meth! How is that possible? The American Council for Drug Education explains that while "illegal drugs can be more rapidly addicting than alcohol and may well have a more powerful effect on human behavior … the high level of alcohol consumption, which is many times greater than the level of illegal drug use, makes it one of America's most serious drug problems." [7]

Alcohol has been called "the most commonly used addictive substance in the United States" [8] and is so powerful that some experts are calling it the real "gateway drug," more so than marijuana! [9] Not long ago, one social worker who deals with drug and alcohol cases told me if she can get a person off alcohol, she can almost always get them off their drug addictions because alcohol is the real stronghold.

In spite of how marketing presents it or how society likes to think of it, alcohol has a definite and strong chemical impact on human beings; and the Christian position becomes a whole lot clearer as soon as we get honest about that.

Let's admit something else: People drink alcohol for more than thirst or flavor. They use it as the drug it is, for the following reasons:

- To calm their nerves.
- To relieve stress.
- To help express themselves.
- To build up their courage.
- To get others and themselves into a casual mood.
- To "liven up" a party.
- To get instant comfort from inner turmoil.
- To forget painful memories.

Many who would never consider themselves as having a drinking disorder turn, nevertheless, to alcohol at decision time. They feel it helps them process their problems. This is dangerous because people begin using alcohol more and more for this purpose. "I need a drink" soon becomes their default for dealing with the least bit of anxiety.

College students tell one another that drinking alcohol is the grown up thing to do, but they are only fooling themselves. They are actually after the effects of the liquid drug (not to mention the chance to be in the "in" crowd). For one thing, students want to drink and want to be around others who drink because alcohol makes taking someone to bed very, very easy.

In 2 Samuel 11, backslidden David used alcohol to get Uriah drunk in the hopes of covering up his adultery with Uriah's wife; and in Genesis 19, Lot's daughters used alcohol to get their father drunk for the purpose of having incestuous relations with him. Alcohol has *always* been recognized as a drug.

CALL IT WHAT IT IS

Christian, let me ask you: Would you take cocaine in moderation? Would you say it would be a marvelous idea to invite your dinner guests to a few puffs of marijuana just to make the evening romantic and interesting? Would you be OK with your 21 year old child taking heroin (just a small amount) to celebrate his or her adulthood? Of course you wouldn't! You know the damage these substances cause. So why consider alcoholic beverages when they are proving to be the biggest addictive hazard of all? "But alcohol is legal and socially acceptable." So what! Are you going to call beer, wine, and liquor by their rightful name—drugs—or are you going to stick your head in the sand like the rest of the world and refuse to see anything more than alcohol's acquired taste and imagined ambiance?

Search for any real, unmistakable endorsement of alcohol in the Scriptures and the only thing you find is the single context of medicinal purposes, clinical drugs. In Proverbs 31:6 and 1 Timothy 5:23, wine is prescribed as a depressant and a treatment for stomach disorder. Actually, I am thankful the Bible (through these verses) speaks to us in these modern times and lets us know that taking medicine is not a sin! I have a pastor friend whose knee was shattered a few years ago. Since then, he has had multiple surgeries and lives in constant pain. He will tell you that the only thing that has kept him sane (and in the ministry) is God's grace and the relief he gets from pain medication.

Drugs have their place; and as a drug, alcohol has its place—but let's face it! People commonly and consistently use alcohol far outside the context of medication and way beyond the boundaries of the Word.

CHAPTER THREE

Some Poor Excuses

Regardless of how it is popularly pitched, the subject of alcohol is not the biblical gray area people make it out to be (as you will see). What is questionable, however, are the excuses and arguments heard among Christian circles. Let me skim over just three of them here.

(NOTE: In the subsequent chapters, I do not use a rebuttal format as I do here. Petty debating turns me off! More importantly, we are told in Scripture to avoid "contentions." What God has given me to give to you is straightforward, solid doctrine. However, when sayings such as the following become constant and obnoxious occasions for turning people from the truth, they then need to be addressed.)

1. In the last chapter, I closed with a mention of 1 Timothy 5:23 where Paul was instructing Timothy not to drink water anymore but to "use a little wine for thy stomach's sake and thine often infirmities." Again, the pure and natural context of this verse is medicinal use, and the Greek word here for *little* literally means "puny."[1] There is nothing here permitting the believer to grab a martini or guzzle a glass of wine. Get real! People who quote this verse as they are "cracking open a cold one" with friends are misusing Scripture—and they are lying! If they were indeed sick, they would most likely be at home taking a puny amount of strong medicine. Truth is, they want a spiritual-sounding pretext for social drinking.

It seems that those who quote 1 Timothy 5:23 are ignorant of the last three words in the previous verse, the directive to "keep thyself pure."

2. In the States (and I would guess elsewhere), you hear people say, "Well, Martin Luther drank." Thank God for Martin Luther and his revelation of justification by faith, but take note that this famous reformer also hated Jews and clearly endorsed anti-Semitism in the Church. Should a person rationalize racial hatred and discrimination simply because Martin Luther or any other heroic figure had prejudice? Of course not!

When it comes to our ultimate behavioral pattern (and specifically alcohol consumption), people are not our final authority. God's Word and the nature of Christ are our law, our tradition, and our reason for doing things. Remember, we alone are responsible for our actions and for what we know to be the will of God, regardless of how others (e.g., pastor, elder, Sunday school teacher, family, friends, cultural icons) have conducted their lives.

3. Along with the European defense I pointed out in Chapter 1, there are a few more popular arguments church people use for drinking, and I have interwoven them in the chapters ahead. This last (and certainly most potent) reason given is, "Jesus made wine at the wedding in Cana." Sounds legitimate at first, but a quick look at the cultural background of this event shows this justification to be untrustworthy and filled with holes—and let me take the next three or so pages to show you what I mean.

A lot has been written about biblical wine. Study it for yourself. It is a fascinating subject. One of the first things I noticed is that in many English bibles, the word *juice* is not used. That is because all gathered liquid coming from the grape is called *wine*, just as it is in Hebrew (although Hebrew has several words for *wine* that indicate its age and even its ingredients). This fact immediately makes the historical biblical study of alcohol complicated as well as controversial.

It turns out that of the 258 mentions of wine (found in 215 verses and which also includes *liquor* and *strong drink*), there are many things highly debatable. For example, some scholars say *yayin* (the generic Hebrew term for wine) refers to both fermented and unfermented wine while others say *yayin* was always fermented to some degree. How wine was made, how it was stored, how it was diluted, how it was reconstituted if it was reconstituted at all, which verses apply to fermented juice and which apply to the unfermented kind—all of these and other aspects seem more or less to be up in the air among scholars. That is why jumping to a conclusion about what Jesus made—either high-alcohol-content *oinos* (the Greek generic term for wine) or plain old grape juice—is wrong!

THREE INDISPUTABLES

To get to the bottom of things, we have to deal with three things that are without debate.

First, we know that in Jesus' day people habitually watered down their wines. In his well-researched article, *Wine in the Ancient World*, Dr. R. A. Baker wrote:

> There can be no argument about whether the ancients diluted their wine; there are innumerable examples from ancient writers to verify this fact.[2]

"What was the ratio of water to wine?" you might ask. Well, now we have another mystery. Some say it was 20:1, others say 8:1. Hirsch and Eisenstein of JewishEncyclopedia.com refer to Rabbi Raba's ancient insistence: "ordinary, fermented wine … be strong enough to take one-third water, otherwise it is not to be regarded as wine."[3] The question then arises, "How consistent was their diluting?" The point is, it remains anyone's guess as to how much water was in Jesus' kind of wine.*

---

* I find it interesting that Jesus' wine was made of water. This, to me, suggests fresh wine or fresh juice of the grape. It is also notable that Jesus said He brought "new" wine to be put in new bottles, indicating freshly squeezed juice that had not been fermented. This wine was compared to the timeworn, strongly fermented Old Testament kind with its tired, stretched out bottles that would not be able to handle what Jesus was serving.

Having said that, the second thing that cannot be argued is the motive that specifically the Jews had for diluting their wine (albeit fresh or old) in the first place: to avoid drunkenness, the sin of Noah. Whatever Jesus made—fermented or unfermented, highly or scarcely diluted—would have complied with this standard.

The third indisputable thing is that God does not tempt with evil (James 1:13). As other writers have noted, the wedding guests had already been doing a lot of drinking. Would Jesus have provided to those at the wedding a beverage that would get them drunk or add to their drunkenness? No, and to suggest otherwise is to say Jesus led the people at Cana into sin. This reasoning applies to the other part of this argument, "Jesus drank wine in the upper room." Jesus would not have indulged in something that would open the door to wrongdoing of any kind, in His life or in the lives of those around Him.

> And ye know that he was manifested to take away our sins; and in him is no sin. (1 John 3:5)

> God is light, and in him is no darkness at all. (1 John 1:5b)

Keep in mind what many Bible-wine authors have noted: that contemporary accessibility to alcohol is far more easy and inexpensive than in Jesus' day; and whereas the ancients diluted their beverages, what people today consume "in cup" is much higher in alcohol content. In addition, our modern stigmas and attitudes connected to alcohol are vastly different from the average Jew of 2,000 years ago.

In short, when all the facts are gathered and perused, the only thing that becomes crystal clear is that the whole matter of drinking today cannot and should not be instantly equated with what was served at the wedding at Cana and the last supper.

NO GREEN LIGHT

Friend, it is a dishonest and dangerous practice to base doctrine, and thereby Christian behavior, on hasty and uncertain interpretation of Scripture. Most of what the Bible says about wine merely states that someone had or drank it, so these verses do not give license to drink. A few verses (less than 15, when last I counted) speak favorably about wine; but even if we knew the exact beverages referred to (e.g., fermented, unfermented, diluted, straight), among these passages is *no exhortation for believers to drink* habitually let alone socially.

A scriptural green light for alcohol simply does not exist!

Some people get hung up on the fact that the Bible does not give us a "thou shalt not drink" directive. Well, neither does the Bible have a "thou shalt not beat thy wife" commandment. Does that mean wife-beating should be presumed acceptable? No! Because of the Scripture's proactive mandates— "Husbands, love your wives" and "as ye would that men should do to you, do ye also to them likewise"—we can unmistakably know the will of God concerning wife-beating and thus can clearly determine our "position" on the issue.

The same with alcohol: what you find in Holy Writ practically condemns or cancels out every aspect of it by virtue of how we are told to behave. In addition, there are dozens of passages that either speak negatively about wine or that outright forbid it; and while I use some of these in the upcoming chapters, what I am most interested in presenting to you are those principles to which the Word obligates us and that are immediately applicable to alcohol. This is where the foggy excuses lift and the valid and vital issues come into focus.

PART TWO

New Testament Mandates

CHAPTER FOUR

Drunkenness

Know ye not that the unrighteous shall not inherit the kingdom of God? Be not deceived: neither fornicators, nor idolaters, nor adulterers ... nor drunkards ... shall inherit the kingdom of God. (1 Corinthians 6:9-10)

It seems that at my home church, the DOOR Fellowship, we have always had a terrific, on-fire youth group—kids who love God in both word and deed.

In the last few years, many of our college-going youth have come back from their various breaks with shocking stories of fellow students who are supposedly Christian but who brag about partying and their drunken conduct. Some of the same kids who our young people witnessed going to chapel and Bible study were also laughing and joking about getting drunk, as if it was no big deal.

I believe the Church is *not* taking the sin of drunkenness as seriously as it ought! Dads and Moms, when is the last time you told your teen what God says about getting drunk? Pastor, when is the last time you preached against inebriation? Drunkenness is nothing to play around with or minimalize! The Scripture specifically says here that people who get drunk are in danger of the wrath of God.

Let me put it a different way: God *hates* drunkenness. How much? In the above verse, the Bible reveals it to be just as wrong, just as corrupt as sexual immorality, idol worship, stealing, greed, rebellion, and extortion. Why shouldn't Christians drink? Because, getting drunk is against the will of God and is something deserving of Hell.

TREATED DIFFERENTLY

Much to Man's shame, we usually do not get strict with sin until it becomes unpleasant to us or when those committing it bring a personal injury or offense. As long as naughtiness and wrongdoing are politely managed and neatly packaged, folks are prone to be apathetic; and that goes for getting drunk. It is only when people begin vomiting, growing violent, or getting out of order that we get upset. Trouble is, God, who is altogether holy, gets upset long before we do.

The Greek word here for *drunkard* literally means "tipsy," which Random House Dictionary defines as being "slightly intoxicated."[1] It does not matter if you can still keep your composure or if those around you think your conduct is normal and acceptable (studies show people have a hard time even realizing when they are buzzed let alone properly drunk[2]). As far as God is concerned, that little "lift" and wobble you feel means you have crossed the line and you are drunk!

If you call yourself a Christian, you should put drunkenness on the same plane as God and the Bible put it. Drunkenness is more than just an embarrassing situation; and it certainly is more than something to be laughed about after others have made fools of themselves. It is the sin of voluntary impairment and just as self-abusive as sticking a needle in your arm. As a believer, getting drunk should be avoided at all costs. So why are so many ministers and church people tolerantly winking at drunkenness within their individual assemblies when God says it's wrong!?

A number of years ago, I was invited to speak at a small church in France. After the service, an elderly sister who was quite influential in the assembly came up to me and began talking to me a mile a minute. I was just beginning to speak French at the time, and of her 15-minute-or-so conversation, I only caught a word here and there. At some point, however, I realized this woman was drunk! Her nose and cheeks were bright red, and they matched the color of her eyes. She had been nipping her homemade wine before service and then afterwards was pouring more for herself and "whomsoever will" (kids included) in the back of the church. Nobody said anything to her, and nobody made any apologies to me on her behalf (though I did not expect they would). It seemed nobody cared she was breaking the Lord's commandments.

TAKE A STAND!

I believe many Christians keep their mouths shut because those getting drunk are close friends, large tithers, prominent church members, or (as in this case) family. I believe another reason pastors in particular neglect to preach about alcohol and drunkenness is because they do not want to sound like an old, fanatical fuddy duddy from a temperance movement. For whatever motive, as long as the brothers and sisters of the Church are silent about drunkenness the problem remains and the sin spreads.

The Bible distinctly tells us how we are to deal with repeat offenders in the church.

> But now I have written unto you not to keep company, if any man that is called a brother be … a drunkard … with such an one no not to eat. (1 Corinthians 5:11)

Are we taking a biblical stand against drunkenness among believers? Are we keeping this commandment from 1 Corinthians 5? We should! We must! Church members and preachers alike should be confronted when they get drunk just as strongly as when they get caught in fornication, extortion, or stealing from the offering plate.

A HIGH STANDARD FOR ALL

Paul the Apostle gave qualifications for bishops, elders, and (here is something interesting) for older saints, mandating that these who are to exemplify Christianity should "not be given to wine" or "to

much wine" (1 Timothy 3:1-3, 8; Titus 1:7; 2:2-3³).
Those who endorse Christian drinking point to these
verses as proof of moderation, but Paul's tone and
objective in each of these passages contradict this
conclusion. These directives are purely hostile to-
wards wine or alcohol and reflect Paul's charge to
the Ephesians, "Be not drunk with wine" (Ephesians
5:18). In other words, if the apostle were to have
used modern vernacular, he might have said, "I don't
want you getting tipsy on Friday and Saturday and
then come in preaching and prophesying on Sunday.
I don't want a bunch of drunks leading the church!"

Incidentally, I have found there are a sizeable
number of church members who think it is OK for
them to live one way, but that their pastor and other
church leadership should "hold to a higher standard." This is untrue! God does not have two sets of
rules: one for the clergy and one for the laity. Those
whom God has called to be examples are to live out
the lifestyle *all believers are supposed to live* but at a
higher profile and with heavier consequences! Bishops should not be greedy of filthy lucre because this
is the requirement for *all* believers. Deacons are not
to be "doubletongued" because this is the standard
for *all* Christians. Seasoned saints are not to get

drunk because this is the Word of the Lord to *all* who call on the Name of Jesus.

PRIVATE DRUNKENNESS

Let me make something else abundantly clear. God has not forbidden drunkenness only as practiced in public. Private inebriation is just as wrong! Some of you reading this book think that just because you can "handle your liquor" in public, you are OK; but as a brother in the Lord I am warning you here and now: For the Christian, the seriousness of drunkenness should never be measured only by how much or how little it bothers others. It makes no difference if your kids are asleep or if you lock yourself in the shed when you get tipsy. *God hates drunkenness,* and regardless of where or when you get drunk, it is a sin!

Would we make the same excuses if we found out fellow members in our church were committing adultery "without disturbing anyone" or if an elder was praying to Hindu idols "in private?" Absolutely not!

Since I mentioned having a seemingly strong resilience to alcohol, read what the National Institute of Alcohol Abuse and Alcoholism has to say:

Often [people] are unaware that being able to "hold your liquor" isn't protection from alcohol problems, but instead a reason for caution. They tend to drink more, socialize with people who drink a lot, and develop a tolerance to alcohol. As a result, they have an increased risk for developing alcoholism.[4]

This puts me in mind of the Scripture about a haughty spirit coming before a fall (Proverbs 16:18). It appears those who take pride in having a large drinking capacity have trouble on their hands, trouble that will bring them down one way or the other.

ON PARTYING

It is not just the act of drunkenness that is sin. 1 Peter 4:3, 5 equates "banqueting," that is, drinking bouts and drunken carousals with the sins of ungodly Gentiles. In other words, if you are thinking about attending a drinking party or going to a bar, don't! The Lord says, "Be not among winebibbers" (Proverbs 23:20a)" and,

Woe unto them that rise up early in the morning, that they may follow strong drink; that continue until night, till wine inflame them!

50

And the harp, and the viol, the tabret, and pipe, and wine, are in their feasts: but they regard not the work of the LORD, neither consider the operation of his hands. (Isaiah 5:11-12)

Our opening Scripture does not just apply to alcoholics. Anyone who becomes intoxicated is living in sin; and unless they repent and stop getting drunk, they will never receive or enter into the Kingdom of Heaven. So if (as someone frankly put it) "drinking leads to drunkenness," why should you even start?

CHAPTER FIVE

Self-control

P aul ordered—not asked—Christians to know how to possess their "vessels in sanctification and honor," stating that this is both the will of God and our "sanctification" (1 Thessalonians 4:3-4). Paul said of himself:

> But I keep under my body, and bring it into subjection: lest that by any means, when I have preached to others, I myself should be a castaway. (1 Corinthians 9:27)

Peter instructs us to give "all diligence" to add "temperance" or self-control to our lives (2 Peter 1:5-6). James tells us to marshal our tongues in order that we may be able to "bridle the whole body" (James 3:1-5). Paul preaches self-control saying that we ought to bring "into captivity every thought to the obedience of Christ" (2 Corinthians 10:5). The

Lord wants you to manipulate your entire person for the glory of God. Get your emotions under control! Bring those motives in line with the cross of Christ! You are called to be a self-motivated child of the Most High who knows how to make yourself do the will of God—and with a zealous attitude.

Alcohol is the enemy of self-control. Remember what you read two chapters ago: it only takes 90 seconds for alcohol to begin affecting your entire system. Proverbs 23:31-32 warns

> Look thou not upon the wine when it is red … [for] at the last it biteth like a serpent, and stingeth like an adder.

I have known many who claimed to be "mature enough" to handle their drink of choice. As long as they were not taking off their clothes or crawling under tables, as long as they had a designated driver they viewed themselves as being "responsible drinkers." Besides, they claimed they had begun drinking just to make meals more romantic, to commemorate festive occasions, and … well, have a beer or two with a few adult friends. Then without warning, the snake struck and the adder stung! Suddenly, they were reaching involuntarily for the bottle, and they became oblivious to how often they were sneaking a "nip" here and taking a "snort" there. Even when they were indulging with others, it never dawned on them that they had begun drinking more than ever and that they were looking forward to alcohol more often and with more anticipation. Soon, the same ones who boasted of having the upper hand over the adder of alcohol watched in a stupor as their lives crumbled before them. I have seen it, and I imagine you have also—all too often.

This puts me in mind of a personal story.

RUSSIAN ROULETTE

From ninth grade on, I attended a medium sized Christian school. Unfortunately, not all of my class-mates had dedicated themselves to Christ, and there was one group of older students who (unbeknown to parents or teachers) got together on weekends to drink. Among those of us in the high school, it was rumored that one drinker in particular (an impetuous kind of guy to begin with) used to go crazy when he would drink. People said that one thing he used to love was playing Russian roulette: you know, the daredevil game where you put one bullet in the pis-tol, spin the cylinder, put the barrel to your head and pull the trigger. Apparently, this guy thought it was hilarious that he could get away with the insanity of beating the death-defying odds.

About a year or two after I graduated, the rumors about my classmate and his "tanked-up" antics were verified. I will never forget hearing how he had been with a bunch of drinking buddies and, after a few beers, how he started his old life-of-the-party stunt again. This time it was not funny. That first chamber held the bullet that killed him.

Here is a horrible example of the power of alcohol. It can make you do things you would never do in a sober frame of mind—things you hate and despise, things that bring you shame and grief, things that destroy your most precious relationships; and bizarrely, alcohol can make you do them all again! Tragically for my former classmate, alcohol made him do something he would never have attempted without his "liquid courage," and eventually something he would never be able to duplicate.

EASY TO LOSE CONTROL

If God forbids drunkenness, it is because He demands we exercise self-control. Many Christians, sadly lacking in basic doctrinal knowledge, are unaware of this; but listen, dear Christian, being a person of disciplined behavior is not just for military-type people or more reserved personalities. Having control over yourself at all times is a clear and unbending biblical commandment.

I have often heard people who drink say that they end up having more alcohol than what they had planned. A truly godly woman, whom I have known since I was a teen-ager, testified recently that, years ago, she and her Christian husband used to drink in private at meals. "At some point," she said, "I began to realize that I could not just have one drink. I had to have two or three, and many times I would feel a slight buzz before I would stop. That's when I knew I needed to quit drinking altogether."

A few years ago, I was talking to a pastor in Belgium who told me that before his conferences he had to take extra steps in notifying attendees that alcohol consumption at the church event was strictly prohibited. The visiting pastors had been getting drunk at the meals between meetings!

Many people (believers and nonbelievers alike) think they can or will quit drinking when they have had enough, that their sense of control will automatically kick in—and this is where they get fooled. People are drinking a substance without realizing the magnetic, beguiling power it can have over them.

You have heard the lame excuse, "The devil made me do it?" Well when it comes to alcohol, that is perfectly true. The Bible says, "Wine and new wine take away the heart" (Hosea 4:11). Alcohol has a way of making your strongest convictions seem so insignificant and making life's consequences seem so far from you. It weakens your willpower, however strong it is when you are sober; and (figuratively speaking) alcohol makes it a million times easier to say "yes" to the wrong things and "no" to the right things.

> And take heed to yourselves, lest at any time your hearts be overcharged with surfeiting, and <u>drunkenness</u>, and cares of this life, and so that day come upon you unawares. (Luke 21:34)

How many people mourn about what they said or the way they behaved after "having one too many"— and all before complete inebriation? Come on! This sort of thing is far from a rare situation. Wild and outlandish drama is common to bars and pubs! Just the other night, we were in a "family restaurant" (as the apologetic waitress later reminded us) when a couple of grown men burst out of the separated bar area and began swinging at each other. Everywhere

58

we see people relinquishing control to a drug—and may I point out that *alcohol always encourages ungodliness*. It never brings you closer to Jesus or fills your heart with brotherly love or involuntarily makes you do the right thing!

CAUGHT UP IN THE CULTURE

All of this trouble with alcohol gets enhanced by the atmosphere of the times. We live in a culture that glorifies unrestrained behavior and that vilifies a decent, conscientious lifestyle. Sinners today want you to tell them right is wrong and wrong is right. Dangerous and foolish as it is, the popular habit is to rebel against common sense and stability; *but don't you be fooled*! "Letting yourself go" and "living it up" is utterly un-Christian—a lifestyle and a liking that is downright sinful. On this, the Bible is clear.

Let us walk honestly, as in the day; not in rioting [carousal, letting loose] ... (Romans 13:13a)

This know also, that in the last days perilous times shall come. For men shall be lovers of their own selves, ... incontinent [*Greek word here means "powerless, without self-control"*

G2970]… lovers of pleasures more than lovers of God; having a form of godliness, but
denying the power thereof: <u>from such turn
away</u>. (2 Timothy 3:1-5)

And [they] shall receive the reward of un-
righteousness, <u>as they that count it pleasure to
riot </u>in the day time. (2 Peter 2:13a)

In Ephesians 5:18, the reason God gives us the
commandment "be not drunk with wine" is because
drunkenness leads to "excess," the opposite of safe,
healthy, and godly conduct.[1] God firmly tells us to
stay in charge of what we are doing. Never hand over
the reins to some glamorous, good-times chemical!

CHAPTER SIX

Sobriety

I f God wants you to have self-control, it is because He is calling you to be sober and sober minded. Please take a look at the following:

> Therefore let us not sleep, as do others; but let us watch and be sober. (1 Thessalonians 5:6)

> But let us, who are of the day, be sober, putting on the breastplate of faith and love; and for an helmet, the hope of salvation. (1 Thessalonians 5:8)

> Wherefore gird up the loins of your mind, be sober, and hope to the end for the grace that is to be brought unto you at the revelation of Jesus Christ. (1 Peter 1:13)

But the end of all things is at hand: be ye therefore sober, and watch unto prayer. (1 Peter 4:7)

Be sober, be vigilant; because your adversary the devil, as a roaring lion, walketh about, seeking whom he may devour. (1 Peter 5:8)

There are other passages which preach sobriety, but I chose these specifically because the English words "sober" here (1 Peter 4:7 "watch") use the Greek word *nepho* which Strong's literally defines as "to abstain from wine!"[1]

Why shouldn't Christians drink? Because, one of the required characteristics of a believer is to be sober. This is just as imperative as prayer, forgiveness, truthtelling, or gathering to worship the Lord with the saints.

OVER DOING IT

Yes, there are some religious sects that forbid entertainment of any kind and seem to equate even smiling and laughing with sin; but this is not Jesus! God has given us plenty of things to enjoy in this life, deeply and fully. The Bible says that one of the fruit of the Spirit is joy (Galatians 5:22) and that the joy of the Lord is our strength (Nehemiah 8:10). Christian, God wants you to have not just any old joy, but *His* joy in your heart—*and there is joy in serving Jesus*!

What becomes sinful and necessary to be avoided is when Christians use their "liberty for an occasion of the flesh," when we cross over into realms of carelessness and recklessness, sacrificing God's principles, our sensitivity to His Spirit, and wisdom itself for cheap, momentary pleasures and for taking foolish chances.

Do you realize there are people today who have laughed their way into eternal damnation? Rather than exercise discernment, they used the excuse that they simply wanted to get out of life all there was, to "live it up"—and alcohol played a key part in fulfilling their resolution.

Keep in mind the quotation from Chapter 2 concerning what researchers have documented, that alcohol "lowers inhibitions and allows the user to relax … to the point of not considering the consequences." Soberness is essential in your Christian walk because not everything labeled "fun" is wholesome, innocent, or helpful; and a lot of what people call "having a good time" is nothing less than sinful indulgence.

Here is something to get you thinking: Did you know it is possible to be too optimistic and too enthusiastic as a believer? When Judah was threatened by war and hostile takeover, all the prophets of Jeremiah's day were prophesying victory over Babylon and crying, "Peace, Peace!" God's complaint was that this spirit and message of hopefulness was entirely void of the most urgent need: complete, practical, heart-felt repentance. "They have healed the hurt of the daughter of my people slightly," was the Lord's protest, meaning that these eager prophets were only injecting cheap pain killers instead of dealing with the actual sickness.

I know churches that can shout, dance, and declare the victory, but they miss the timing of God and move of the Spirit because they fail to discern when they ought to be "rending their garments" and crying "between the porch and the altar." Revelation's church of Laodicea was like that, and Jesus said He would "spew" them out of His mouth …

Because thou sayest, I am rich, and increased with goods, and have need of nothing; and knowest not that thou art wretched, and miserable, and poor, and blind, and naked. (Revelation 3:17)

GOOD-TIMES GOSPEL

Here again, we have to be careful that our culture of partying and lawlessness remains filtered out of our doctrine. When we as the Church seek only good times and want to hear only good things, we are in danger! Micah faced a spiritual dilemma that sounds so familiar to us in the twenty-first century:

> If a man walking in the spirit and falsehood do lie, *saying,* I will prophesy unto thee of wine and of strong drink; he shall even be the prophet of this people. (Micah 2:11)

Apparently, anyone prophesying about bountiful crops and great booze became a church celebrity; and that is what is happening now! Ministers are telling people whatever they want to hear, including that drinking and partying are totally fine, just so long as you do not embarrass anyone or get into legal trouble. Jesus said of the last days:

> For there shall arise false Christs, and false prophets, and shall shew great signs and wonders; insomuch that, if *it were* possible, they shall deceive the very elect. (Matthew 24:24)

There are many things in this life you have to check for authenticity, and preachers are one of those things! The devil sends out his ministers as charming, passionate personalities who are fond of saying, "It is written," but who deliver teachings that strongly appeal to your flesh and fleshly thinking. If you let up from being on your toes—using godly discernment and guarding against "enticing words"—you can easily be deceived. Why else does the Scripture say, "Examine yourselves, whether ye be in the faith" (2 Corinthians 13:5a) and "believe not every spirit, but try the spirits whether they are of God" (1 John 4:1)? You must be continually sensitive to the voice of the Holy Ghost and thoroughly unshakeable in Bible beliefs. You must be sober.

CLEAR THINKING NEEDED

Call me whatever names you want, but I have to stand up and let you know that drinking is no automatic "given" to Christians. There are serious and substantial reasons why you should stay away from alcohol, and one of them is because alcohol takes a certain edge off your soberness or your performance as a believer. The Scripture clearly warns:

It is not for kings, O Lemuel, it is not for kings to drink wine; nor for princes strong drink: Lest they drink, and forget the law, and pervert the judgment of any of the afflicted. (Proverbs 31:4-5)

They also have erred through wine, and through strong drink are out of the way; the priest and the prophet have erred through strong drink, they are swallowed up of wine, they are out of the way through strong drink; they err in vision, they stumble in judgment. (Isaiah 28:7)

Aren't we New Testament believers called to be kings and priests unto God? Yes, we are! Therefore, we are called to stay sober. There are commandments to be remembered, judgments (that is, decisions) to be made, and a vision of the Kingdom that deserves our full attention.

God is serious about this business of staying vigilant and sharp, and He says:

Woe unto them that are mighty to drink wine, and men of strength to mingle strong drink [*and here comes the reason for the woe as well as the result of the action*]: which justify the wicked for reward, and take away the

righteousness of the righteous from him!
(Isaiah 5:22-23)

I repeat: As a son or daughter of God, the Lord
wants you to have clear thinking constantly. Don't be
naïve, brothers and sisters. Serving God takes con-
centration. You have to put praise over persecution,
faith over fear, and devotion over emotion. You have
to know how to pray when it seems you do not have
a prayer, and you have to exercise sound judgment
and see things for what they actually are—because
like fun, not everything labeled "Jesus" is Jesus.

CHAPTER SEVEN

Don't Give Room to These

As a Christian, you have three constant foes: sin, flesh, and the devil. Before you were saved, these things were your friends, so to speak; but these friends you loved and adored so much led you into paths of death and separation from God. Now that you have accepted Jesus, you are free from the shackles of these old back-stabbing oppressors; however, let no one tell you differently: It is possible after having "escaped the pollutions of the world through the knowledge of the Lord and Saviour Jesus Christ" to be "entangled therein, and overcome" (2 Peter 2:20). You must, therefore, war against what used to be so familiar and comfortable to you—and there is one thing you need to know and remind yourself over and over again.

Sin, flesh, and the devil (Hell's Big Three) have one thing in common: They are severely deceptive.

They can make the most heinous evil appear attractive, innocent, and indispensable. The Bible has plenty of examples of strong and godly people who, becoming lax and full of pride, became deceived by them.

Repeatedly Scripture warns us:

Let not sin therefore reign in your mortal body, that ye should obey it in the lusts thereof. (Romans 6:12)

Dearly beloved, I beseech you as strangers and pilgrims, abstain from fleshly lusts, which war against the soul. (1 Peter 2:11)

Neither give place to the devil. (Ephesians 4:27)

GUARD AGAINST THE FLESH

I have written about this before, but we have to remember that we who are flesh and blood (believers though we may be) have a pre-resurrection default. Paul calls it the Law of Sin (Romans 7:23), and he said:

70

... with the mind I myself serve the law of
God; but with the flesh the law of sin. (Romans 7:25b)

For the flesh lusteth against the Spirit, and the
Spirit against the flesh: and these are contrary
the one to the other: so that ye cannot do the
things that ye would.(Galatians 5:17)

In other words, if ever and whenever we let down
our guard and stop living by the Spirit, we will automatically resort to practicing sin.

There was a certain friend of mine whom the
Lord had gloriously saved and delivered of alcohol
as well as drugs. He was an eager and hungry young
Christian who eventually became an influential
leader in the church. At one point, he felt particularly
strong about going into the ministry and expressed to
me a deep desire to see Christians come into the
fullness of Christ, but something happened.

Somewhere along the line he allowed lukewarmness and carnality into his life, and one of the first
indications that this young man was straying was his
sudden announcement to church members that he
thought there was nothing wrong with drinking.
When we confronted him about the change in his
lifestyle, he assured us he would never head back to

his former habits (how often we have heard that). He said he simply liked the taste of beer and was approaching alcohol from a more mature standpoint (there is that word "mature" again). All the arguments everyone uses, he used, including that he had no intention of backsliding.

Well, he left the church and is back to his old ways which include smoking, swearing, gambling, and drinking (not just beer or wine but hard liquor); and regardless of his promise, he is getting drunk—all because he underestimated the powers of his fleshly lusts.

Friend, we should *never* resort to trusting our flesh! You can theorize all you want about Christians reaching some impervious plateau, but the disastrous proof of what spiritual carelessness does is universal. When believers start trusting their experience, their position within the Church, their seniority as a believer, their personal testimony, their biblical knowledge—when they become wise in their own eyes, they will fall! We can allow no sense of accomplishment or sophistication to bring us false comfort, *let alone a liquid drug* which pacifies our flesh and makes us feel pleased about whatever we do and say.

"THERE IS NO GOD"

I will never forget being in the hospital for a severe case of kidney stones. The doctor had prescribed a strong pain medication which was to be given to me whenever I felt even a slight throbbing, and I remember the warm and numbing feeling the drug gave me as soon as the first dose was injected. At one point as I lay in that hospital bed, the thought came to me, "There are no problems in life, and there is no God."

Where did that thought come from? I can tell you, it did not come from my spirit or my heart because as soon as it came I said to myself, "Wait a minute! I love the Lord, and I know that life has its problems." Yes, you could say it was the drug, but that thought came from my flesh as it was under the influence of the drug. *The drug simply amplified my flesh.*

We talked about self-control, but what are we to control? Our flesh! Every day of your Christian life you will have to battle with your flesh, and it has been my observation that you will battle your flesh much more than the devil himself.

I hear many preachers complain about how more and more of their church members are becoming carnal and engaging in social drinking. Well, let me ask you, dear fellow minister: when is the last time you preached to your people that they must crucify their flesh and bring it under subjection, that Christ enjoins them to "die daily" and to take up their cross? If people are reaching for the can and the bottle more than ever, if alcoholism is becoming a greater problem in the Church, it is because the pulpit is silent where the Bible is evident and forceful.

ALCOHOL AND THE DEVIL

You read earlier that the devil "walketh about, seeking whom he may devour," and that means you have to be on guard for more than the lusts of your flesh. Satan is on the prowl, too; and like sin and flesh, the devil is devious. He does not play fair, and he does not come to you and say, "I'm Lucifer, and I'm gonna do such and such so I can ruin you." No! He comes as an angel of light (2 Corinthians 11:14). Never get lazy. Never assume that just because you had victory over the devil in the past, you now have perpetual immunity.

A few weeks ago, my youngest brother, Matthew (who is a dynamic preacher), was at our church in one of the rooms working after hours on a project.

Suddenly, a young man appeared in the doorway (one of the elders invited him in) and asked "Pastor Matt" if he could have a few moments to speak to him. Naturally, my brother welcomed him, and the two began to talk.

The young man (whom we had known from a few years before as someone who wanted nothing to do with Jesus) began relating how the devil was troubling him, and how alcohol was directly connected with his experiences. This guy said he was in the habit of drinking whiskey till he blacked out, and after a while both he and his drinking girlfriend began seeing dark spirits on a regular basis.

In line with what the book of Proverbs states about alcohol,[1] my brother said, "Man, you are drinking the spirit of snakes."

"I know! I know!" the young man said. "I feel that all the time!"

"Are you drunk now?" my brother asked a few times.

"No," was the repeated response.

Finally, Matthew said, "Well if you are ready to leave your old lifestyle and get right with God, I'll pray for you right now in Jesus' name, and I believe you are going to get delivered."

The young man said he wanted deliverance and raised his hands. Matthew started praying, and in a few moments the power of God came on this alcohol-loving guy. A noticeable and glorious change came over him. Jesus had brought deliverance!

Matthew and the young man stood there worshipping the Lord for quite awhile (you would, too, if you felt Jesus in the room!), and at one point the young man said, "I feel so different." Suddenly, he dropped to his knees and then fell on his side, overwhelmed by the presence of God.

Up to this point, Matthew said he smelled no alcohol on this guy's breath or clothes, but as soon as the young man hit the floor the room filled with the scent of liquor. God was detoxing him right there!

TAKE THIS SERIOUSLY

Moses called the wine of the heathen "poison" (Deuteronomy 32:33), and this is exactly how I would describe the effect alcoholic beverages have on individuals today. These drinks do more than simply go down into your stomach, like soda and fruit juice do. They get down into your soul and your spirit. How pained I am to see those who once burned with the Holy Ghost have their flame doused by alcohol!

The night of Jesus' arrest, He said these words, "For the prince of this world cometh, and hath nothing in me" (John 14:30b). Herein should be your ambition, for God has called you to follow Jesus' example, to "put on" the same Spirit that is of Christ and "make not provision for the flesh" (Romans 13:14a). Beloved, take holiness and soberness as seriously as God does.

> Abhor that which is evil; cleave to that which is good. (Romans 12:9b)

CHAPTER 8

Lust

A number of years ago, the leadership from a prominent church in our area got the "revelation" that Christians could "take a little wine for the stomach's sake." The pastor, his wife, and couples from the assembly began going to bars together. In the beginning (like always), it appeared to be a pleasant, responsible evening with all of them; but it was not long before the predictable happened. Episodes of adultery (within the group and otherwise) began taking place, the pastor being one of the participants! The shameful news exploded in our city and beyond, bringing a reproach to the Gospel. Families in the congregation were devastated and many left the church, some people backslid, the youth group went ballistic, divorces ensued, and today the church no longer exists.

Know what happened? After a glass or two of alcohol, these "mature" believers would get romantic (a natural side-effect of alcohol). Somebody suggested dancing, "with spouses" of course; but soon, the couples were swapping partners on the dance floor—"It's OK as long as my husband or wife is here." Flirting followed, then more drinking—but with the new companions. You can guess the rest.

SUDDENLY AND UNEXPECTEDLY

You will recall that Proverbs 23:32 talks about wine biting like a serpent and stinging like an adder. Verse 33 tells one of the ways alcohol suddenly and erratically strikes:

> Thine eyes shall behold strange women, and thine heart shall utter perverse things.

Without planning it, without meaning it, and even without being properly drunk, your chemically stimulated mind will revert to and intensify your God-given reproductive penchants.

Somebody will say, "Well, I've been drinking for years and neither my friends nor I have had affairs or have taken a stranger to a hotel." That is praiseworthy, but let me ask you: Does this commendable characteristic of you and your group *guarantee* others will stay out of a bed of fornication? No! Should you recommend alcohol to other Christians *based solely* on your experience? Of course not! Let me also remind you, my friend, that your past performance *in no way* protects you from future slip ups of your own.

Christians make a colossal error when they justify alcohol by using hypothetical situations ("what if" scenarios which prove and ensure nothing) or, as above, by using irregular, singular results as their conclusion. As to the above statement, drinking and self-restraint is *not* the norm. There is an undeniable link between alcohol and sexual sins, and the evidence is everywhere!

IT'S PART OF THE PACKAGE

It is no coincidence that commercials for alcoholic beverages and places which serve them feature scantily-dressed, suggestive females. The debaucheries of our colleges' spring breaks are always accompanied by drinking. To many, "partying" automatically refers to an event with alcohol and "hot" people. The term "one night stand" is almost exclusively used for two strangers who first meet at a bar. What about country and western music? It is famous for singing about drinking that is followed by going to bed with somebody who is not your spouse; and if people like these kinds of songs, it is because they can personally identify!

On a violent note, the National Institute of Alcohol Abuse and Alcoholism writes, "Approximately one-half of all sexual assaults are committed by *men who have been drinking alcohol.*[1] Several studies found that child sexual abuse experiences for both men and women were associated with *family histories of alcoholism.*"[2]

Have you ever heard the term "beer goggles?" Wikipedia gives this definition, "A slang term for the phenomenon in which consumption of alcohol lowers sexual inhibitions to the point that very little or no discretion is used when approaching or choosing sexual partners."[3] Earlier this year, the London newspaper, *The Independent*, showcased the experience when it ran the article "Scientists Solve the Mystery of How Beer Goggles Work."[4]

Again, I am ashamed to say that, in my experience, the people who deny alcohol's link to lewdness are loophole-seeking church goers! They care almost nothing about the facts. They hardly care about the biblical warning. Instead, they are bound and determined to indulge—but just ask the world. They will tell you straight out (though in crude terms): alcohol makes lust easy, excusable, and mutual.

DRINKING MAKES IT EASY

In her brochure entitled, *Real World Drinking*, Ruth Mahang (MA, MPH) warns college students, "People take more sexual risks when they've been drinking."[5] Even after just one or two drinks, people feel comfortable giving their bodies to strangers and acting like the tramps and sleaze bags they condemn others as being. As a drug, the soothing effect of alcohol hypnotizes you, in a way, causing you temporarily to forget the importance of your commitments, whether they are to a husband, a wife, a fiancée, or even God!

Ladies, did you know women get drunk quicker than men? According to an article by Dr. Jason Kilmore, "If a man and woman who are the same size drink at the same rate, the woman will get more drunk."[6] In other words, you are more vulnerable to losing your self-control than a man. Taking advantage of you becomes less difficult with every sip of your alcoholic beverage, *and do not think men are unaware of this fact*!

Adultery and fornication will take you to the Lake of Fire, but remember: it is more than the *act* of immorality that is abominable to God. Under the higher standards of the New Testament, even allowing and retaining the *thought* of sexual misbehavior stirs up divine wrath, because as far as Jesus is concerned:

> ... whosoever looketh on a woman to lust after her hath committed adultery with her already in his heart. (Matthew 5:28)

Lust must be highly guarded against, even when you are sober. Nevertheless, that flirtatious conversation, that seductive look, that slight but uncalled for touch—all the allurements and possibilities of fornication become effortless and normal-feeling when alcohol is part of the mix.

CHAPTER NINE

Temple of the Holy Ghost

As a Christian, you are no longer a vessel of wrath into which or from which come the filthy, weird things of darkness, and you certainly are more than just a warmed over sinner. Because of the shed blood of Jesus, you are a saint, and you need to see yourself as such. After all, God tells you in His Word that you are now to serve Him with your whole person—including your body, for He calls your body "the Temple of the Holy Ghost" (1 Corinthians 6:19). Before you were saved, you were more or less indiscriminate as to what you did with and to your physical being; but now that you have been changed (and are still being changed), you have something to protect and to cherish, something far better than gold, "yea, than much fine gold:" God's own precious presence, though that treasure be in "earthen vessels."

All the reasons I have given you up to this point lead to this: You need to be concerned with what you do with your body. It is not enough to worship God in just your heart or your mind. There are tangible, functional deeds that either qualify or disqualify you from being a true worshipper. The Bible says the body is for the Lord and the Lord is for the body (1 Corinthians 6:13). God wants to come to you, His temple, and find a clean and holy place to inhabit. He wants to find a heart atmosphere that is pure, not just in the sense of passion but also in the sense of participation. The Bible says:

> Keep thy heart with all diligence; for out of it are the issues of life. (Proverbs 4:23)

How do you "keep" your heart? Get involved and stay involved with things and people that are true, honest, just, benevolent, of good reputation, and worthy of praise (Philippians 4:8). God has separated you from those who live for their own pleasures and lusts. Now, you have the privilege and the right to live according to God's will.

I wish more Christians understood this, because Christianity does not work and does not make sense if you are living for yourself—regardless of the emphasis by modern church doctrine!

EXCLUSIVE DEVOTION

So what does this have to do with alcohol? First of all, we talk about how fornication creates a "soul tie" between two people (*see* 1 Corinthians 6:13-20); well alcohol creates its own kind of soul tie with the drinker. I think I am safe in saying that, for the most part, people don't drink because they are truly thirsty (especially these days with all the waters and sodas available). As we saw back in Chapter 2, alcohol becomes the go-to substance for people, their daily drug. Alcohol is their comforter, their strength, and their guide; and the trouble is, what people are seeking to experience from the bottle or the tap is what should be sought for at the face of God! People are not being filled with the inspiration of the Holy Ghost. They are being filled with the stimulation of a chemical, one which feeds their flesh and their devotion to flesh; and again and again they faithfully resort to this liquid fellowship.

God refuses to live where there is split devotion. If the dynamic of His indwelling presence and the experience of His power take a less-than-exclusive priority in your life, if you look forward to the sensations and incidents that come from the drug called alcohol, if the subculture of drinking is putting things in your heart and cluttering the courts of your soul, then the Spirit of God will simply depart, leaving you alone to defile your temple! Sorry, but God does not wait around to compete with anything or anyone. He is an all-or-nothing Master.

In the tabernacle worship God established by Moses, priests were forbidden to drink any kind of wine (fermented or not),[1] and God commanded this so that those who ministered in that man-made, temporal place would retain a personal sense as well as a general atmosphere of sacredness. In Christ, we have a better testament *and* a better tabernacle. Should we not, therefore, show more respect and devotion for the present dwelling place of the Lord? Is not Jesus worthy of the purity affected by our sobriety, our self-control, and our full attention?

> But I say unto you, That in this place is *one* greater than the temple. (Matthew 12:6)

WHO IS IN CONTROL?

A few weeks ago I heard a young man testify, saying that the Scripture God gave him for staying away from alcohol was the one I cited above concerning our bodies being temples of the Holy Ghost.

I have heard many others come to this same conclusion: alcohol (along with drugs and cigarettes) is wrong for the obvious reason that it inflicts excessive and unnatural harm to the physical body, and that it brings potential addiction, which makes our spiritual temple unclean and disgraceful.

This, of course, makes perfect sense and is a viable and worthy motive for abstinence; however, I believe something can and should be added to this conclusion. After all, it is more than just the potential physical harms that make this a sin against our bodies. The other factor is the motives behind drinking.

The world still operates under the old Tower of Babel spirit: you *have to* join us, and you *have to* do things our way. When it comes to alcohol, there is enormous pressure put on people to drink, and this should tell us right there that something is diabolically wrong! Again, people do not drink alcohol primarily because they suffer thirst. One major reason they drink is to fit in and be accepted by the crowd.

Drinkers don't like to see people in their company with an empty glass or a hand without a bottle. They want everyone indulging because they feel threatened otherwise. I know drinkers who have chal-

89

lenged nondrinkers publically, saying something like, "You're trying to be better than everybody. Come on! Loosen up. Have some fun." The question for the Christian is: who is going to rule your life and make your decisions for you: the crowd or the Holy Ghost?

INTIMIDATION

I knew a Christian guy who was working in the Washington D.C. area at a prominent law firm. He was young but showed incredible talent and promise to the owners, so they promoted him. Everything was going fine until one day the owners called my friend into the office. They had no complaints about his work; it was his personal life with which they had a problem. "We've noticed that whenever we take you out for dinner, you don't drink." The young man said he was a Christian and for that reason he did not partake. His answer displeased the owners. "If you intend on staying in our firm," they said, "you had better learn how to drink and how to serve alcohol to our clients. We don't want our clients feeling uncomfortable."

The young believer stuck by his convictions and left the firm. Thank God for courageous saints; but here is yet another case where people force alcohol, making it top priority—even over faith. Drinkers do not want to see you, the abstaining Christian, remain sober. They want you to join them in getting tipsy and drunk so they can obtain appeasement for their ways.

> Woe unto him that giveth his neighbour drink, that puttest thy bottle to him, and makest him drunken also, that thou mayest look on their nakedness! (Habakkuk 2:15)

I have known of several cases where "sipping saints" mock, intimidate, and threaten fellow church members who do not drink, blasting them with accusations like, "You're just being judgmental and holier-than-thou!" I know of indulging ministers who do the same thing to their abstaining colleagues—and you have to wonder: what spirit is behind all this coercion, which disregards the convictions and consciences of Christian brothers and sisters *whose abstinence harms no one nor spreads any sin*? It certainly is not the Spirit of Christ! Such bullying only strengthens my own persuasion of how much alcohol encourages the flesh and works against the things of God.

PLEASING GOD

The revelation of being the Temple of the Holy Spirit means that your life—your spirit, soul, and body—is to bring glory to God, but it also means you are ultimately focused on pleasing the Lord *and only Him*. Jesus said:

> No man can serve two masters: for either he will hate the one, and love the other; or else he will hold to the one, and despise the other. (Matthew 6:24a)

Galatians 1:10 says if we please men, we are not the servants of Christ. If we are constantly bending and reshaping our lives just to placate others, inevitably we *will* sacrifice the principles of God *and even the presence of God*! If anything should be disposable to us, it should be man's approval and having a reputation of being cultured or cool.

As the temple of the living God, you are *supposed* to be separate. You are supposed to be different. No, it is not a matter of being different for difference sake; it is a matter of being led by the Spirit of God instead of by the spirit of the age. You are God's property, and the Bible says the only thing you really owe other people is to love them.

Let's be honest, many people only consider drinking in the first place because they "fear the face of clay." If your whole reason for drinking is to alleviate peer pressure—albeit on a collegiate level, a professional level, a social level, or even on a family level—you are putting man before God, and you are more interested in being a popular temple than a spiritual one!

CHAPTER TEN

Appearance of Evil

The moment you get saved, unbelievers begin a close inspection of your life. Unfortunately, many watch because they want you to make a mistake so they can ridicule you and justify their own lifestyle; therefore, never give unbelievers an occasion to criticize the things of God. This is the Bible mandate found in the following verse. It is not that the Kingdom is so frail that poor public perception is going to bring it down. It is simply because even a "questionable" Christian reputation hinders full impact of God's truth. Careless behavior can and does turn people away from coming to the Christ of Calvary and the empty tomb. Besides, there are other sinners who watch your behavior because inwardly they want to know if Jesus and Christianity are real.

As a believer, you are a Gospel ambassador and it is your duty to be concerned with how others view the Kingdom. You cannot afford to do whatever comes into your head or whatever whim sparks your desires. Scripture raises awareness of this when it instructs,

Abstain from all appearance of evil. (1 Thessalonians 5:22)

STIGMA

I cannot speak for other parts of the world, but here in the United States, establishments such as bars, clubs, and cocktail lounges have a generations-long stigma. Like it or not, the general public sees these as being places for wild behavior, picking up bed partners, and getting high as well as stone drunk; and believe me, unbelievers will tell you outright and unashamedly that they look forward to going to their favorite "watering hole" and to living up to its reputation.

I was in Scotland earlier this year, and a couple of police officers attended the church in which I ministered. Thinking on this subject, I asked the officers separately what they found to be the number one problem in their area. Alcohol was their instant and definitive answer. One dilemma the police are facing there is that people (young and old) are getting utterly drunk on the weekends and causing all kinds of trouble. The officers told me about a popular saying which goes something like, "If I don't remember what I did, I had a good weekend."

In my travels to Europe, Africa, Central America, the Middle East, as well as throughout North America, I have recognized that alcoholic beverages *themselves* have a universal reputation. Root beer, ginger ale, lemonade, and similar drinks simply do not get the same reaction from people as when somebody cracks open a can of beer or pops a bottle of champagne. With alcohol comes a dramatic dynamic in the atmosphere—and never a Christian one!

Subsequently, when people (especially sinners) see you walking out of a store with a six pack of beer, they think "party." When people see vodka, gin, or whiskey in your grocery bag, they think about getting drunk. Wine is a bit different, that is true. It has both a high class status as well as a laid back one (depending on where you are drinking it)—but do not kid yourself! Everybody still equates wine with the risks and motives of the rest of the alcohol family. The bottom line is: people simply do not look at alcoholic beverages as being completely harmless or innocuous—and as a Christian that should alert you!

WHAT THEY REALLY THINK

It makes no difference how you excuse alcohol as it is being poured into your glass. Your unsaved friends may smile, nod their heads, and seemingly agree with your "liberty" as a Christian; but at the end of the day, those who drink to get drunk, who drink to pick up women or men, and who drink to do all the other wicked stuff associated with alcohol are going to equate your behavior and motives with theirs. The stigma will stick. I have seen it happen more than once; and more than once, I have heard unbelievers tell me, "That guy says he's a Christian, but I don't think he is. He drinks."

Someone will say, "I've been drinking for years, and I don't know of anyone I have hindered from getting saved." How about the waiters and waitresses who serve you alcohol? How about the people tending you at the bar or pub? How about the clerks who ring you up at the liquor store? Has it ever occurred to you that they know you though you may not know them? It is a great possibility that you have enabled them with a horrible excuse, "They are Christians. So if they drink, so can I." Keep in mind that these observers most likely will have little or none of the cautions you might; and what makes matters worse is you will never know the effects of your actions on the ungodly until the Day of Judgment; but then, it will be too late to reverse what you have done.

Ironically in this age of moral madness, people are looking for standard bearers, real-life heroes with honorable convictions who will not bend to social pressures as they have. Oh, they would never readily admit this. It is much more convenient for them to keep step with the crowd and mock you, a principled person, in public while admiring you in private.

Your "no" to alcohol can be a working testimony of your faith and your personal integrity.

CHAPTER ELEVEN

The Greatest of All

P aul had a quandary, a "gray area" he had to deal
with in the church at Corinth. It seems the
saints there were split over whether or not it was
right to eat meat offered to idols.

One side held the position that heathen-dedicated
meat linked a person to idolatry, a sin in which many
in the congregation had undoubtedly been involved
with before converting to Christ. If the church had a
good copy of Old Testament Scriptures, this faction
most likely would have stood on verses about how
much God hates the worship of idols. They would
have undoubtedly pointed out commandments
against eating "unclean" animals, which was a typi-
cal and well-known part of pagan ceremonies. Of
course, this side had a legitimate argument; but the
other side had a viable one, too.

Obviously there were others in the congregation who also had been idolaters before getting saved but happily declared they were free by the power of God, *completely* free. This group probably emphasized the power of Jesus' blood as well as the fact that they were new creatures, starting life from scratch with a fresh and Heaven-corrected consciousness of what was right and what was wrong. It seems they maintained a mantra: that meat was meat, regardless of what some idolatrous priest did with it. This "yes side" felt nothing wrong with sitting down in public and eating what the "no side" deemed as polluted; and they probably felt that total abstinence was, in a sense, fearing or giving attention to a god that was not a god, something they wanted to avoid.

In his letter to the Corinthians, Paul appears to have favored the "freedom-to-eat" view point. At least, that is the theme with which he began his address to the assembly. God is God, Paul asserted, and He, not the idols, provides all meats. However, Paul had no intention of ignoring the serious and holy disdain for idolatry. Years later in the Apostle John's revelation, Jesus would rebuke the church at Thyatira for eating "things sacrificed to idols" (Revelation 2:20); and this standard was in Paul's spirit as well, for he instructed those at Corinth to "flee from idolatry" (1 Corinthians 10:14). The church would trust and follow whatever Paul decided—that was not the struggle. There was something else in the heart of this venerable Jewish apostle that he had to take into account.

THINK LIKE CHRIST

Paul had been raised very strictly with scores of rules; but additionally, he had been trained to observe those rules, especially the extra-biblical ones, with no questions asked and with no explanations given. As it is now, so it was then. A just-do-it-because-I-said-so environment may create compliance, but only a superficial sort. No doubt, Paul realized after coming to Christ how shallow his former spiritual state had been, despite his strong theological upbringing.

The Holy Ghost inside Paul wanted to do more than issue to the Corinthians a thou-shalt-not-eat-that-meat edict or, for that matter, a do-whatever-you-want license. The Lord wanted the saints to exercise their spiritual senses, to put on the mind of Christ and see this dispute from a godly viewpoint, not a carnal one. So under divine inspiration, Paul wrote what now speaks volumes regarding our present question of alcohol.

> But take heed lest by any means this liberty of yours become a stumblingblock to them that are weak. For if any man see thee which hast knowledge sit at meat in the idol's temple, shall not the conscience of him which is weak be emboldened to eat those things which are offered to idols; And through thy knowledge shall the weak brother perish, for whom Christ died? But when ye sin so against the brethren, and wound their weak conscience, ye sin against Christ. Wherefore, if meat make my brother to offend, I will eat no flesh while the world standeth, lest I make my brother to offend. (1 Corinthians 8:9-13)

Here is Paul's finale to the meat debate, and here is the ultimate motive for staying away from alcohol: *brotherly love*! Take a look at this passage:

> It is good neither to eat flesh, nor to drink wine, nor any thing whereby thy brother stumbleth, or is offended, or is made weak. (Romans 14:21)

Wow!

The text is clear.

CARE FOR THE FLOCK

I believe every previous reason I have given you from the Scriptures is legitimate and indispensable, but this eighth one continues to bring awe to my soul. Paul bypassed all the petty claims everyone was presenting (the pros and cons) and got to the root: if our participation in an event or practice causes another Christian—that is right, *a Christian*—to fall or to backslide, God counts our action as a sin against us!

Jesus cares for those who are still tender in their faith; and as the Great Shepherd, He continues to watch out for the welfare of the entire flock of God. Jesus is so concerned that believers help and not hinder one another, He says:

> But whoso shall offend one of these little ones which believe in me, it were better for him that a millstone were hanged about his neck, and *that* he were drowned in the depth of the sea. (Matthew 18:6)

If your drinking *or your stated approval of drinking* leads to someone getting drunk, behaving in an ungodly manner while under the influence, fornicating while under the influence, becoming an alcoholic, or any other alcohol related sin, *God holds you as both a cause for and an accomplice to that sin!*

I have heard people say concerning drinking, "I've got rights and freedom as a believer. Why should I care what anyone thinks?" You should care because it is the loving thing to do. It is the Christ-like thing to do! As Paul commands:

> Let no man seek his own, but every man another's wealth. (1 Corinthians 10:24)

I have heard other people say, "Well I drink and I don't feel any conviction whatsoever. It doesn't bother *my* conscience." Perhaps not, but as a person who is called by God to conform to the image of Jesus, questions about behavior should *never* be decided by your personal preferences alone. The first thing to consider is the principles of the Word, and after that:

> Conscience, I say, not thine own, but of the other: for why is my liberty judged of another man's conscience? For if I by grace be a partaker, why am I evil spoken of for that for which I give thanks? Whether therefore ye eat, or drink, or whatsoever ye do, do all to the glory of God. Give none offence, neither to the Jews, nor to the Gentiles, nor to the church

of God: Even as I please all men in all things,
not seeking mine own profit, but the profit of
many, that they may be saved. (1 Corinthians
10:29-33)

Even if you do not *want* the responsibility, there
are people looking to you for direct or indirect leadership concerning drinking: new converts, believers
who are former alcoholics, those who are struggling
at the moment with doubts or despair, and let's not
forget about all the impressionable young people in
the Church. On top of that, there are in practically
every congregation the traumatized victims of alcoholic parents, mates, and children who bear indelible
emotional scars. Do you consider what your actions
do to them, or do you break out the booze anyway?

According to the Apostle Paul, many in the
Church today have it entirely wrong: Christian maturity is *not* how close a person can get to the gray
areas and remain in one spiritual piece. For that matter, being able to rationalize one's conduct is certainly no mark of growth or tenure, let alone a
justification. Christian maturity is all about selfless,
Christ-like love, for God and for man!

Knowledge puffeth up, but charity edifieth. (1
Corinthians 8:1b)

107

CHAPTER TWELVE

Bonus Reason

W hy shouldn't Christians drink? Allow me to give you one more reason and tie all of this together:

> And this I pray … that ye may approve things that are excellent. … (Philippians 1:9-10)

If I have been stern in this book, it is, for one thing, because of the subject itself. Alcohol is doing serious and pervasive damage outside as well as inside the Church. A lot of what this liquid drug does can be found in studies and reports but, in my opinion, most of its horrors and harm slip past statistical notice. As noted, I have seen the devil use alcohol in order to take advantage of people, decimating their lives with every drop.

On the other hand, my bluntness comes because I hear an urgent and desperate cry of the Holy Spirit going out to the Church, "Arise, my people! Do those things that are excellent!"

My heart grieves because too many in the Church look only for what is passable and marginal. They try pushing the envelope to see how much they can get away with, how far they can go from the norm of Christianity, and how close to the world they can get. Many times I have heard people make rhetorical challenges like, "So you're saying that if I have one beer I'm going to Hell." Always, this has woefully indicated to me far more than a position someone takes on the single issue of alcohol. I have recognized from such mouthy statements the unhealthy and defective heart condition of yet another church minimalist throwing in the towel, settling for less than Jesus' standards, and allowing the enemy to neutralize them.

The danger is, when you wrestle with the Word of God, twisting the Scriptures to find loopholes, looking for the supposed gray areas to which you can run, 1 Peter 3:16 says this will be to your own destruction!

Fellow Christian, I long to see you grow strong in the Lord and "in the power of His might." I want to see congregations walk honorably before God and receive all Heaven can give. I want to see the entire

Body of Christ turn our world upside down for the sake of the Gospel—but God only pours these excellent things into and through excellent vessels.

Here is something noteworthy: *Alcohol is a nonessential*! To me, this clear-cut perspective is what makes all the excuses for drinking all the more exasperating. Sports events, family reunions, weddings, holiday meals, vacations, and all the rest do not have to be associated with booze. You can get along successfully and extremely happily in life—and even more so—without drinking one drop of alcohol.

Listen, my friend: Like sin, drinking never corrects itself. In 2010, Health Magazine had an article showing that not only are more Americans drinking these days, but like in the U.K. and Europe, binge drinking is also on the rise.[1] How dare we treat alcohol, one of the worst and most extensive problems of our times, in a nonchalant manner just because we like a little bubbly with our candlelight dinners!

Rebellion is so popular these days. Well, instead of defying parents and authority figures, how about rebelling against something worthy of resistance and mutiny? We need to protest and resist what alcohol is doing to our families, our friends, our culture, and our churches.

God calls you to be a person of excellence in Christ Jesus. So when it comes to drinking, the question to ask is: If you know that alcohol is a "dangerous" drug, if you know it constantly causes severe problems, if you know there is a risk of getting tipsy (let alone getting all-out drunk), if you know you may lose some or all self-control, if you know your Christian sobriety can be compromised, if you know the enemies of your soul may be given a foothold, if you know you could become even somewhat alcohol dependent, if you know lust is made easier, if you know there is a stigma with alcohol, if you know you could turn sinners and saints alike away from Jesus and full-fledged devotion—what is the safest, wisest, and best thing to do!?

There is only one answer: do not drink.

In the end, we who follow Jesus are to live for the glory of God. That, and not self-centered desires, is our maxim. May it be said of us as it was of our precious Lord and Master, "He hath done all things well" (Mark 7:37b).

112

Endnotes

1. Alcohol is a Problem

[1] NIAA, *Alcohol Use Disorders*, as of September 21, 2012, http://www.niaaa.nih.gov/alcohol-health/overview-alcohol-consumption/alcohol-use-disorders

[2] Dr. Deborah S. Hasin; Dr. Frederick S. Stinson; Elizabeth Ogburn, MS; Dr. Bridget F. Grant (2007, July) American Medical Association. *Prevalence, Coorelates, Disability, and Comorbidity of DSM-IV Alcohol Abuse and Dependence in the United States*, pg. 7

[3] National Council of Alcoholism and Drug Prevention, FAQ/Facts, as of November 5, 2012, http://ncadd.org/index.php/learn-about-alcohol/faqsfacts

[4] WHO, *Global Status Report on Alcohol and Health*, 2011.

[5] Centers for Disease Control and Prevention, *CDC/NCHS, National Health Interview Survey, 1997– June 2010*, as of November 5, 2012, http://www.cdc.gov/features/ds5drinks1day/

[6] (Hingson and Kenkel, 2003) Full cite: Hingson, Ralph and D. Kenkel. *Social and Health Consequences of Underage Drinking*. In press. As quoted in Institute of Medicine National Research Council of the National Academies. Bonnie, Richard J. and Mary Ellen O'Connell, eds. Reducing Underage Drinking: A Collective Responsibility. Washington, DC: The National Academies Press, 2003.

[7] WHO (2006). WHO Facts on Alcohol and Violence, *Child Maltreatement and Alcohol*, pg. 1

[8] CDC staff (2011, October 4). Centers for Disease Control and Prevention. *Press Release: CDC report shows about 112 million annual incidents of people drinking and driving*, as of September 21, 2012, http://www.cdc.gov/media/releases/2011/p1004_drinking_driving.html

[9] NHTSA (2012, April). NHTSA's National Center for Statistics and Analysis, *Traffic Saftey Facts: 2010 Data*, pg. 1

[10] (NIDA, 2008) Full cite: National Institute on Drug Abuse. "*Volume 1: Secondary School Students*, National Survey Results on Drug Use from The Monitoring the Future Study, 1975-1997. Rockville, MD: Department of Health and Human Services, 1998.

[11] Costs related to substance abuse include treatment and prevention, medical care, police, fire department, adjudication, and sanctioning expenses,as well as property damage and related expenses associated with crime, motor vehicle crashes, and fires involving alcohol. (Harwood & Bouchery, 2001) Miller, T. and Hendrie, D. Substance Abuse Prevention Dollars and Cents: A Cost-Benefit Analysis, *DHHS Pub. No. (SMA) 07-4298*. Rockville, MD: Center for Substance Abuse Prevention, Substance Abuse and Mental Health Services Administration, 2008.

[12] D.J.W. (2011, April 26). Every Fifth German Has a Drinking Problem. *The Local*, as of September 20, 2012, http://www.thelocal.de/society/20110426-34631.html

[13] Deutsche Well staff (2007, November 13). Excessive Drinking Growing Problem in Germany. *Deutsche Well*, as of September 20, 2012, http://www.dw.de/dw/article/0,,2902258,00.html

[14] Rachel Ryan (2006, November 18). The Highs and Lows of Germany's Drinking Culture. *Deutsche Well*, as

of September 20, 2012,
http://www.dw.de/dw/article/0,,2226609,00.html

[15] News-Medical.Net staff (2005, November 28). "Alcoholism - The Simple Truth" – France, *News-Medical.Net*, as of September 20, 2012, http://www.news-medical.net/news/2005/11/28/14713.aspx

[16] Bouthoorn, Selma H.; van Hoof, Joris J.; and van der Lely, Nicolaas. *Adolescent alcohol intoxication in Dutch hospital centers of pediatrics: characteristics and gender differences*. Springer-Verlag, 2011. As of September 20, 2011,
http://www.iumsp.ch/Enseignement/postgradue/medecine/doc/JC03052011.pdf

[17] As of September 21, 2012,
http://www.direct.gov.uk/en/CrimeJusticeAndTheLaw/CrimePrevention/DG_181558

[18] Institute of Alcohol Studies (2010, July 29). IAS Fact Sheet, *Alcohol and Crime*. pg. 6

[19] Scottish Government (2012) *Framework for Action: Changing Scotland's Relationship with Alcohol*, pg. 26

2. Alcohol is a Drug

[1] *Make a Difference: Talk to Your Child About Alcohol*, U.S. Department of Health and Human Services, National Institutes of Health, National Institute on Alcohol Abuse and Alcoholism. pgs. 3, 4, 10

[2] The University of Lethbridge (2006, January 11). How it Affects You: Your Body, *Alcohol Awareness*, as of September 22, 2012, http://www.uleth.ca/alcohol/affects.html

[3] Buddy T (2012, June 18). Why You Should Never Drink and Drive, *About.com Guide*, as of September 25, 2012, http://alcoholism.about.com/od/dui/a/impaired.htm

[4] Nick Gilmore, Risk Reduction Program Coodinator for the Army Substance Abuse Program (2012, August 23). FH Alcohol Offenses on the Decline. *The Fort Huachuca Scout/Areotech News*, as of September 20, 2012, http://www.aerotechnews.com/forthuachuca/2012/08/23/fh-alcohol-offenses-on-the-decline/

[5] "Announcement of the 1999 National Drug Strategy," White House News Conference, February 8, 1999

[6] Elizabeth Flock (June 21, 2012). U.S.News & World Report, *Chart: What The DEA Refuses To Admit About Drugs*, as of November 5, 2012,

http://www.usnews.com/news/blogs/washington-whispers/2012/06/21/chart-what-the-dea-refuses-to-admit-about-drugs

[7] American Council for Drug Education, as of November 5, 2012, http://www.acde.org/common/alcohol.htm

[8] National Council of Alcoholism and Drug Prevention, FAQ/Facts, as of November 5, 2012, http://ncadd.org/index.php/learn-about-alcohol/faqsfacts

[9] Steven C. Webster (2012, July 5). Study: The 'Gateway Drug' is Alcohol, Not Marijuana, *The Raw Story*, as of September 21, 2012, http://www.rawstory.com/rs/2012/07/05/study-the-gateway-drug-is-alcohol-not-marijuana/

3. Some Foolish Excuses

[1] Strong's Greek Dictionary, oligos, 3641

[2] Dr. R. A. Baker (2007) "Wine in the Ancient World", as of September 25, 2012, www.churchhistory101.com/docs/Wine-Ancient-World.pdf

[3] As of September 25, 2012, http://www.jewishencyclopedia.com/articles/14941-wine

4. Drunkenness

[1] Chicago Manual Style (CMS): tipsy. Dictionary.com. Dictionary.com Unabridged. Random House, Inc. http://dictionary.reference.com/browse/tipsy (accessed: September 26, 2012).

[2] NIAAA (2010). National Institute on Alcohol Abuse and Alcoholism, *Rethinking Drinking: Alcohol and Your Health*, NIH Publication No. 10-3770, pg. 3

[3] Notice that in verse 2, the aged men are to be "sober." This word comes from the root *nepho*, which means "to abstain from wine." See Chapter 6 for more.

[4] NIAAA (2010). National Institute on Alcohol Abuse and Alcoholism, *Rethinking Drinking: Alcohol and Your Health*, NIH Publication No. 10-3770, pg. 3

5. Self-Control

[1] See Strong's Greek Dictionary, G810

6. Soberness

[1] See Strong's Greek Dictionary, G3525

7. Don't Give Room to These

[1] Proverbs 23:32

8. Lust

[1] Dr. Antonia Abbey; Tina Zawacki, M.A.; Philip O. Buck, M.A.; A. Monique Clinton, M.A.; and Dr. Pam McAuslan (2001). NIAA, *Alcohol and Violence*, Vol. 25, No. 1, pg. 44. Italics mine.

[2] Ibid., Dr. Cathy Spatz Widom with Dr. Susanne Hiller-Sturmhöfel, pg. 53

[3] Wikipedia.org (article updated 2012, September19). Alcohol and Sex, as of September 28, 2012, http://en.wikipedia.org/wiki/Alcohol_and_sex#.22Beer_goggles.22

[4] Rodger Dobson (2012, April 1). Scientists Solve the Mystery of How Beer Goggles Work, *The Independent*, as of September 28, 2012, http://www.independent.co.uk/news/science/scientists-solve-the-mystery-of-how-beer-goggles-work-7606251.html

[5] Ruth Mahang (1998, Reviewed 2007). ETR Associates, *Real World Drinking*, Title No. R746

[6] Dr. Jason Kilmer (2000). ETR Associates, *Drinking Facts*, Title No. R843

9. Temple of the Holy Ghost

[1] Leviticus 10:9

12. Bonus Reason

[1] Denise Mann (2010, July 20) More Americans Drinking (Alcohol), *Health.com.*, Health Magazine, as of September 22, 2012,
http://www.cnn.com/2010/HEALTH/07/20/americans.drinking.alcohol.study/index.html

For BibleDays books and more,
visit the author's website
www.bibledays.org

Want to email?
contact@bibledays.org

DOES THE BIBLE TEACH PERFECTION?

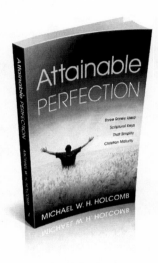

Yes, but not <u>your</u> kind of perfection. Hey! That's good news!

Three keys that will help you come to maturity in Jesus Christ.

<u>Available at</u>
www.bibledays.org
www.amazon.com

IN PAPERBACK OR EBOOK!

Not on the internet? Send $17.50 to:

BibleDays Ministries
PO Box 2515
Williamsport, PA 17703